CW00357530

Whip
Your
Life into
Shape

Take charge, free your
spirit, and become the
mistress of your life with
the Dominatrix Principles

Whip
Your
Life into
Shape

Emily Dubberley

Andrews McMeel
Publishing

Kansas City

06 07 08 09 10 SSI 10 9 8 7 6 5 4 3 2 1

Conceived and produced by

Elwin Street Ltd.

79 St. John Street

London, EC1M 4NR

www.elwinstreet.com

ISBN-13: 978-0-7407-5458-6

ISBN-10: 0-7407-5458-0

Library of Congress Control Number: 2005921791

Illustrations by Joe Berger

Printed in Singapore

Contents

7 Taking control of you

33 Taking control of others

65 Taking control of love

89 Taking control of your life

112 Index

Taking control
of you

We all know her. The woman who always appears to be completely cool, calm, and in control of her life. The one who is friendly, charming, witty, and intelligent. Who has a great career, home, relationship, and time for a social life. Her va-va-voom is down to something that money just can't buy. It's all thanks to something she's tapped into, something we call her Inner Dominatrix.

Your Inner Dominatrix

The dominatrix is envied, admired, and desired. She is assertive and commanding. She gets what she wants and lives her life to her own rules, effortlessly controlling her home, her work life, her finances, and the people she meets. Using the dominatrix principles, you can take control of your world and release a new you. Every woman has a being who is adventuresome and powerful, from the bedroom to the boardroom. With the dominatrix principles you can learn to unleash your inner domme at any time to achieve exactly what you want from your life.

What Do You Want From Her?

Perhaps you have the perfect career, but can't get your home in order. Or maybe you're surrounded by a loving family, but really need to take charge at work. Maybe you're after more time to yourself, or even just more time, period. Whether you need your domme every day or just to get you through the toughest times, once you have her in your sights you'll realize the strength she can bring to every experience.

Domme's Dos & Don'ts — Releasing Your Domme

What's it about?

✓ It's about believing in yourself, your abilities, and what you can achieve.

✓ It's about knowing that anything in life is possible.

✓ It's about taking control for yourself and of yourself in every aspect of your life — from playing the game to paying the bills.

✓ It's about a sassy glint in your eye and a fire in your heart.

✓ It's about being cool without being cocky, strong-willed and sexy, feisty but friendly and fun.

✓ It's about realizing that woman inside of you, and loving her.

What's it not about?

✘ It's not about a world of whips, chains, and bondage.

✘ It's not about being arrogant and intolerant to other people's wants, needs and opinions.

✘ It's not about being intimidating and humiliating others.

✘ It's not about being pushy and shouting to get your point across.

✘ It's not about demanding change in others without considering change in yourself.

✘ It's not about being bossy — just the boss of your world.

The Dominatrix Principles

Seductive, powerful, nurturing, sensuous, delicate, decisive, intense, forceful, in charge — these are all words well known to the domme and are often used to describe her impact on the world. Effective dominance comes from the core, and no amount of power dressing can make a domme out of a woman who hasn't worked on her power and grace by following the principles below.

Honesty

The domme knows clearly what she wants and deals honestly with pleasure as well as with her limits and displeasures. She sets boundaries gracefully so that others want to respect them.

Confidence

A woman in tune with her inner domme understands that the ultimate power comes from genuine self-confidence. The confident woman simply knows she's awesome.

Humility

The domme understands that she must be humble as well as awesome. Humility, the knowledge that she is not superior to others, has a calming effect, bringing her an air of grace and elegance that is so alluring.

Timing

The strongest woman always understands when to release her domme, when to rein her in, and when her domme isn't needed at all.

Independence

A strong woman is not defined by her domme, nor by how others react to her. She is defined by a sense of self and comfort in her own identity.

Decisiveness

The domme knows to approach situations with decisiveness. Each decision is committed with mindfulness, whether based on instinct, conscious thought, or sound advice.

Persuasion

Dommes know that the ultimate power is that of persuasion not fear or force. To get others to willingly, even happily, do for you what you command of them.

Respect

The woman in touch with her domme knows the value of respect. Of giving it and of receiving it. She knows how to command it and, most importantly, not to fail to show it to others. Without respect, there is no leadership. Without leadership, there is no dominance.

Role-Play

To help your inner domme spring free, you need to walk a mile in her kinky boots, and the easiest way to do this is by role-play. Don't panic — you don't need to don those boots, a rubber dress, and brandish a whip. Instead, just spend a day as a shinier, foxier you.

Raid a friend's wardrobe for clothes that you'd never normally have the guts to wear. Check with her that they're flattering to you — a good pal will be honest — and before you leave the house, repeat to yourself "I am strong, confident, and going to have a fantastic night."

Pick a venue that's outside your normal comfort zone — in domme character, you'll have the guts to fit right in, no matter where you are. Whether it's somewhere sophisticated, trashy, or trendy, by setting yourself a challenge — and rising to the occasion, which you will — you're opening yourself up to new and positive experiences. Once you get to your destination, step through the door, pause for a few seconds, smiling and casually scanning the room, and only then walk in. You'll automatically project confidence by not cowering at the door as if you have no right to be there.

If you want to go the whole hog you could even change your name for the night. But then again, why bother? A confident woman will simply reclaim her born name and make it represent everything that makes her feel strong.

Accessing Your Domme

First, picture your inner domme. Does she look like you? Speak like you? Think about the qualities she's got that you admire. Then look at the list below and see how many of the statements you agree with:

- I often leave conversations thinking
  "I wish I'd said . . . Why didn't I say . . . ?"
- Sometimes I feel I'm doing things just to please other people.
- I regularly find myself thinking "How did I get into this?"
- I prefer other people to take the lead in most areas of my life.
- I rarely feel appreciated, and often feel worthless.
- I often say "yes," when I really mean "no."

Now consider how many your domme would agree with. Far fewer, yes? She would never agree to something she doesn't want to do. She would please herself. She would take the lead, and say what she feels, and get what she wants. And achieve this without hurting feelings, damaging friendships, or causing others to feel let down.

So how do you find your Inner Dominatrix? There are two steps. The first, and easier, works from the outside-in and involves dressing the part, then acting the part — putting your domme on like a costume, then behaving accordingly. To help establish your contact with your domme, and to tune in to her in record time, choose an object or objects that get you into the right frame of mind — a particular pair of shoes or piece of underwear, certain makeup or piece of jewelry — and wear them as you practice her.

The second step is a deeper, more difficult one, and works from the inside-out. This requires an inward probing for that beneath-the-surface domme who is more than just a friendly support. This domme needs nurturing and focus, but is then with you whenever you need her. Your inner domme will only reveal herself when she knows you are

Whip Workshop
Creating Your Domme

To find your domme, nominate famous dominant women with whom you identify. Your list may contain women of mythology, history, and media such as Venus or Medusa, Boadicea or Cleopatra, Condoleezza Rice or Margaret Thatcher, Marlene Dietrich or Mae West, Madonna or Gwen Stefani.

Then list pure archetypes — stereotypes you visualize as dominant: the exacting teacher, the strict governess, the severe Mother Superior. Take those elements from each that you identify with, then mix them up with female role models from your own personal history who have had a positive influence, perhaps a favorite aunt, godmother, teacher, or friend.

Visualize your finished domme who draws power and influence from this distinguished list. She is the embodiment and epitome of power for you.

willing to submit, look honestly at yourself, and stand up for what you want. The confident woman inside doesn't believe in kidding yourself. If you try to fool her that you're happy when you're not, it'll be bye-bye, baby.

The Three Selfs to Success

The best way to access your domme is to acknowledge that there are some personal changes you need to make that will ultimately give you more control. Once you've accepted this, whipping your life into shape will come a lot easier. However, these changes can never be accomplished if you don't abide by the "three senses of self" — the three major components that make up your inner domme. She can't be accessed until you've accepted that these feelings lie inside of you; without them, she's powerless.

Self One — Belief

Let's start with self-belief. You can only really believe in you when you stop comparing yourself to other people. To achieve this, concentrate on your own life. Don't waste any time worrying about the things you see around you that you

"Everything's in the mind. That's where it all starts. Knowing what you want is the first step toward getting it."

Mae West
Actress and sex symbol

think are better than what you have now. Don't look at the world around you and place yourself at a certain level. The level you choose will inevitably be too low. Even enlightened women still struggle against the tradition of being quiet, passive, submissive, and gentle. Self-belief does not mean that you have to relinquish gentleness and calm. Only that you have the right to speak and be acknowledged about things that affect your life.

A quiet dominance should instill in others a sense of respect and a desire to please. Finally, accept that beauty is not custom-designed, manicured nails, Gucci shoes, or perfect hair and makeup. Beauty is confidence, grace, posture, and presentation.

Self Two — Control

Self-control is being in charge of your body, mind, and actions. It's about understanding your emotions and reacting to situations and people in an appropriate manner. You may wonder how you can gain control when life can be so unexpected. You can't preempt or prevent every situation, but a domme takes steps to make life work better in general, so that when the unexpected happens she has the emotional and physical space and strength to deal with it.

So, from the beginning, let's assess the day-to-day routines. Most of us fall into a routine — no matter what age we are or how our lives are. It makes our days less stressful and provides a cushion against the pressures of each day. All too often these

"It doesn't matter who you are, where you come from. The ability to triumph begins with you. Always."

Oprah Winfrey
Entrepreneur and talk show host

routines come about by chance, the demands of others, or lack of thought, rather than by design. For example:

- You sacrifice going to the gym before work because you have to drive your partner to his office.
- You always get your lunch from the same store because your friend fancies the man who works the deli counter.
- Tuesday evenings you stay in with your oldest friend because that's what you've done since you were sixteen.

You get so used to the routine that you forget to question whether your days are passing as you really want them to. And that's where your inner domme can help. A woman who's in touch with her confident side doesn't go with what life throws at her if it doesn't make her feel good. She takes charge. She doesn't just let life happen — she makes it happen in a way that suits her.

Self Three — Confidence

Self-confidence is about having faith in your abilities and knowing that anything is possible. "It's that buzzy feeling that helps you deal with your self-doubts, sees challenges as opportunities, and ultimately, it gives you the courage to go for whatever's going to make you happy," says Susan Quilliam, author of *Positive Thinking*. Once you have a little self-belief and self-control, the confidence comes naturally — it's maintaining it that can be difficult.

Confidence isn't a steady state and you have more of it at some times than others. But how do you hold on to those "I'm so great" feelings? Most people whose confidence is shaky find it tough to focus on their good points. They usually get into the habit of concentrating on all the negative things about themselves, but to build your self-esteem you have to do the opposite. The more you focus on building your feelings of brilliance — in all aspects of your life — the more easy access you'll have to your confidence when you're challenged.

Start with your posture. Submissive girls tend to stoop, trying to take up as little space as possible and make as little impact as possible. A domme walks tall, unafraid to make her mark on the world. So, head up, shoulders back, stomach in, and chest out (as an added bonus it also enhances your figure.)

As well as walking with confidence, there are many other ways your inner domme can send out positive body

Domme's Dos & Don'ts — Confident Conversation

What's it about?

✓ It's about leaning toward someone you're interested in to show that you're engaged by what they're saying.

✓ It's about making sure your breathing is slow and controlled before you talk. If you hear your voice speeding up, simply stop and breathe deeply again.

✓ It's about watching to see whether they start copying your posture. If they do, it's a good sign that they like you — and see you as being in charge.

✓ It's about the power of smiling. It's one of the few universal pieces of body language and will show that you're at ease with yourself. A good smile goes up to the eyes.

What's it not about?

✘ It's not about being defensive. Don't block people by introducing barriers like a newspaper between you or crossing your arms.

✘ It's not about speaking too loudly or too quietly in order to dominate the conversation.

✘ It's not about covering up. Don't touch your lips or nose while you talk. The former suggests you're shy about what you're saying and the latter implies you're lying.

✘ It's not about avoiding contact. Don't look down as you chat to someone, or slump in your seat. It suggests you're lacking in confidence or don't enjoy chatting to the person you're with.

language — and get a positive reaction back. Consider your face. Well, more specifically, your eyes. If you want the world to know you're in charge, your eyes can do it for you. The right look can get you pretty much anything. It can get a door held open for you, a round of applause after a presentation, or that last chocolate, so choose your glance wisely. Keep looks direct but friendly.

Next, forget about barrier gestures — you don't need to cross your arms or legs to protect yourself. Let your hands rest casually at the side of your body, and your feet sit comfortably next to each other (no Sharon Stone's, and no cheating by crossing your ankles.)

Always own the space that you're in. If someone starts to infringe on your personal space, speak up and explain that they're crowding you. Unless they are trying to annoy or intimidate, most people don't want to crowd others.

Finally, it's no good looking and acting confidently if you're as shy as a mouse when you open your mouth. Projecting self-esteem can start with your appearance, but it doesn't mean anything if it doesn't carry through to your personality. Planning always helps, but rather than forcing a conversation, steer it with well-timed queries, observations, or references. If you don't want to talk, then don't. But make sure that this is your choice and not dictated by others.

Saying "No"

One of the basic principles for boosting your quality of life, both in and out of the home, is being able to say "no." "This is hard whoever you say it to, but especially when it's to those you care for," says Karen Sullivan, author of *How to Say No and Mean It*. The thing is, they're the ones you have to be the most careful of when it comes to being taken advantage of: the friend who makes you feel guilty if you don't drive for miles to see her; the sister who asks to borrow your clothes but never returns them. It's not that they mean to test your patience; it's just that they know they can get away with it (c'mon, we even bet you've been guilty of it in the past!). But the new you is a self-confident woman who knows that the power of "no" is perhaps the strongest ammunition she needs when it comes to life-whipping, because with it you have the power to please yourself, not just other people.

Learning to say "no" is one of the biggest life-shaping steps you can take. You don't have to turn down everything just because you can, but the more people hear your confident, considered "no," the sooner they'll respect it and accept it without a fuss.

Whip Workshop
Steps to a Confident "No"

- If someone asks you to do something, don't agree to it straightaway. Take some time to consider your answer.

- If you find you want to say "yes" you'll feel happy and content with the idea; if it's "no" you'll already be feeling some resentment at the prospect.

- Make "no" the first word you utter. Then say something direct, such as "I'm not available/it's not convenient/not this time."

- Be pleasant and keep your voice firm.

- A confident woman never gives lengthy excuses as to why she's saying "no" — she knows the other person will try to find solutions to them.

- Suggest alternative solutions: — "No, but perhaps we could get together next week?"

- Stand your ground and don't back down.

- Keep repeating "no."

Setting Boundaries

A domme knows what she wants and goes out to get it — but before you can do that, you have to set your boundaries: where you want to go, what you want to do, how you want to be treated, and what you see as unacceptable.

The biggest hurdle in setting your boundaries is becoming comfortable with articulating what you want — and sticking to it. Many women think that by setting boundaries they're being demanding. They worry that they'll make people feel bad, think that denying their own

Dominatricks

A major trick to saying "no" is to state it confidently at the beginning of your answer. Offering a lengthy explanation that ends with "no" simply signals that "no" is the afterthought rather than the driving point of what you are saying. Whip that "no" out from the very start and let it work for you.

feelings is "no big deal," and as a result, get taken for a ride. But now that you know how to use the word "no," there's nothing to stop you getting what you want.

Saying "I can't" takes a lot more confidence than saying "I can," whether sexually, socially, or professionally. But adhering to your boundaries means you'll get what you want: more time to pamper yourself, less time in the office, or a guy who wouldn't dream of being late for a date.

Domme, Know Your Boundaries

It may sound obvious, but before you can share your boundaries with other people, you need to know what they are yourself. Think about what's important to you. Go with the old-school psychological approach of making a list, then read it every day to reinforce your willpower.

If you love seeing your friends but you spend all your time out with colleagues or acquaintances you're not that close to, use the magic word "no" the next time they ask you out. If you always leave work late because your boss sees you as someone who's constantly available, say "no" the next time they ask you to bind 75 reports at 6:30 P.M. on a Friday. And if your beloved asks you if you'd try that special kinky thing they love but you hate, just say "no." It sounds simple — but that's because it is.

Of course, you may well be struggling with years of conditioning here, but that's where your domme persona can come to the rescue. Being a domme is about control — of yourself as much as the person you're dominating — so take that control. It's your time, your emotions, and your energy that you're wasting otherwise — and a domme respects herself way too much to waste her life. In new situations, set your boundaries from the start. Protect your boundaries ferociously and they'll protect you.

Whip's Words of Wisdom

The next time someone asks you to do something and you're not in the mood, set your domme free. Smile, look them straight in the eye, and say "No, that's not convenient." Soften it if you must, but never with justification, and never with "I'm sorry" or "I apologize" — they might think you're not sure.

Eliminate the Negatives

So where can you use these new skills of saying "no" and setting boundaries? Everywhere! A domme is as strict with herself as she is with other people: she has the balls to strike anything out of her life that doesn't make her feel good. And she's not scared to analyze herself either.

Make a list of all aspects of your life: friends, relationships, money, work, leisure time, spirituality, and anything else that matters to you. Rate each area on a scale of one to ten. If something scores less than ten, write down the reasons why it's less than perfect: does friendship get a low score because you don't get enough emotional support, you feel like you're being taken for granted, or simply because you'd like more friends?

Once you know where the problem lies, it's much easier to fix it, whether that's by chatting to your friends and explaining your concerns, refusing to give in when people ask you to do things that you don't want to, or going out with the aim of making new friends.

Another way to categorize your life and eliminate the negatives is to use Maslow's *Hierarchy of Needs* — a chart mapping what makes people happy. There are five "needs" in the hierarchy: physiological, safety, love, esteem, and self-actualization. The first entails making sure your basic physical needs are met: that you have enough to eat, somewhere to sleep. Safety refers to being protected from physical danger but also feeling emotionally safe and supported. Love is self-explanatory, but also taps into our need to belong. Esteem covers both self-esteem (confidence) and esteem from others. People who have achieved only the first three "rungs" often crave status in the eyes of others, so will wear designer clothes or drive an expensive car. The ultimate rung, self-actualization, is about becoming all that you can possibly be. Work out which rung you're on, and if there's anything blocking your progression up the ladder, eliminate it from your life.

By using your domme attitude to take control of your life and throw anything negative out of bounds, you're well on your way to achieving true happiness.

Time for You

Now that you've whipped the negatives out of your life, you'll find that you've got more time for yourself — so use it. Time alone is vital for your self-esteem. It gives you space to think about your motivations and find yourself without other people distracting you or leading you away from your core. But don't panic — you don't need to sit cross-legged and chant "Om." Just do things that you enjoy.

People with low self-esteem often feel uncomfortable spending time alone because they need attention from other people to prove that they are interesting or worthy of existence. A domme scorns that self-indulgent nonsense, and instead indulges herself in fun ways. It could be by having a long bubble bath (complete with glass of champagne or tub of ice cream). It could be by reading a book, playing a

Dominatricks

If you feel nervous about going out alone, invest in a notebook so you can scribble down your thoughts and look like you're busy. This is also a good way to ward off unwanted advances — just look the person interrupting you in the eye and say "I'm working" or "I'm busy."

computer game, doing a crossword, going swimming, shopping, horse-riding, or visiting a restaurant and enjoying a gourmet meal alone. It could even entail getting on a plane and visiting a country you've always been curious about.

Rather than seeing "alone time" as a negative that means you don't have enough friends, see it as a positive: an opportunity to do exactly what you enjoy without anyone else's demands. The advantage of being on your own is that the only person you need to please is yourself. And don't waste your time on your own just watching TV. After all, you're in the company of someone amazing: yourself.

Dominatips

Your domme will help you to develop your inner strengths and the more you let her free, the greater help she'll be to you. Now let's take the next step to taking control of your life and address the problems that are caused by other people.

Taking control of others

Often other people cause us to veer from our chosen path. From dealing with determined salespeople or figures of authority to making friends and coping with the ones you love. From your in-laws to your boyfriend, your best friend to your children, your inner domme is here to help you cope with everyone around you.

People Pressure

"She doesn't suffer fools gladly" is a commonly used phrase, but a domme doesn't suffer fools at all. And that doesn't just mean people who are obviously foolish. It's any of life's leeches: people who suck up your time, energy, or emotions without giving anything back.

Leeches are good at pressuring submissive girls into doing what they want, whether it's a friend who always coerces you into going to the bar you hate where she fancies the barman, a mother who expects you to spend every Sunday with her, or a salesperson who won't get off the phone when you want to relax and eat your dinner.

A domme refuses to bow to such pressure. She values her own time too much. If someone is trying to pressure her into doing something that she doesn't want to, she'll simply reiterate her boundaries, stand her ground, and keep on saying "no" until the leech gives up.

That doesn't mean that if a friend calls at 4:00 A.M. having been dumped by her long-term lover, she tells her to go away. And it doesn't mean that she refuses to compromise either. A domme not only knows her boundaries but respects

Domme's Dos & Don'ts — Controlling Other People

What's it about?

✔ It's about spending your time with the people you want to, those who add to your life and to your happiness.

✔ It's about managing those people who waste your time. Maintaining your boundaries so that you keep time for yourself.

✔ It's about valuing yourself and your life, not relinquishing your time and your needs to the whims of others.

✔ It's about taking control of your environment, not being bullied or cowed by aggression or coerced by people who refuse to listen.

✔ It's about facing authority figures as equals with calm self-assurance.

What's it not about?

✖ It's not about ignoring friends in need, nor retreating from your family or colleagues.

✖ It's not about bullying or demeaning people you meet, nor being cold and distant, just in case they make demands on you.

✖ It's not about forcing other people to do as you wish or avoiding compromise or discussion.

✖ It's not about looking for trouble.

✖ It's not about being rude.

✖ It's not about refusing to accept that others may know more or have greater experience.

other people's — she won't impose her will on anyone. But if people try to pressure her into doing something that she doesn't want to do, either individually or as a group, she'll stand her ground until they come up with something that's acceptable to her.

A lot of the time, people pressure is socially-related: going to a Thai restaurant because your friends love it, even though you hate it; spending a night in a club that plays music which you find just as audibly pleasing as nails down a blackboard; or going shopping with someone who insists on going to all the designer shops when your budget's more chain store.

A passive girl is more likely to go with the flow and accept any invitations that come her way. That's why she then ends up sitting in her apartment on a Saturday night, wondering why she's got such a boring life — or tagging along with her friends to some club she really doesn't want to go to. A domme takes responsibility for her own social life instead. So, one trick to pull is to start organizing social events yourself. If you've already invited friends out to something you want to do at the weekend, they're less likely to try to foist their ideas upon you because you've got in there first.

It's not only socially that people pressure can come into play. You may encounter time thieves who assume that they need your time more than you do; attention-seekers who refuse to see why anyone other than them should get noticed; or confidence-quashers who have a magical skill of making you feel lousy every time you see them. And you could encounter them at work as well as socially.

Even your family and partner can be guilty of pressuring you into doing things that you don't want. So, set your domme free and get ready to release the pressure in your life, no matter where it's coming from.

Dominatricks

One of the simplest tricks is to voice your desires. Simply tell your friends that you're not into Thai food, or clubbing, or designer clothes. Chances are, they don't mean to make you do things that you don't enjoy, they just figure you're into the same things that they are because you've never mentioned that you're not.

"Leadership is a matter of having people look at you and gain confidence, seeing how you react. If you're in control, they're in control."

Tom Landry
Football legend and coach of the Dallas Cowboys

People Who Steal Time

Time thieves are all too common, but a domme realizes that time is a precious thing, and she's certainly not going to waste it on people who are worthless. Passive women can recognize time thieves by the sinking feeling that runs through their body when they see that person's number flash up on their cell phone display, or their car pulling up into the driveway. You know that, no matter what you're doing, the time thief will beat you into submission and eat into the afternoon you'd planned to spend tidying the apartment or making out with your partner. A time thief

Whip Workshop
Trimming the Time Wasters

Unless there's a reason to have someone in your life, be that emotional or practical, they're superfluous. And a domme doesn't allow anything in her life that has no benefit. And she certainly doesn't feel guilty about eviscerating negative people.

Take out your cell phone/address book. Highlight everyone in there — whether friend, lover, or colleague — who's made you feel good about yourself in the last year, in no matter how small a way. It could be that they bought you lunch when you were broke or that they provided a listening ear when you were feeling bad.

Next, mark important business contacts, your immediate family, and any practical contacts (e.g., doctor, dentist, gynecologist). Now, delete everyone who's left. They haven't added anything to your life in a reasonable time period and, as such, you shouldn't waste your time on them.

doesn't pay any attention to hints: they'll settle down and demand a cup of coffee even if you're clearly in the middle of something else, and any reasonable person would realize that they've picked an inconvenient time.

All too often, time thieves aren't aware of what they're doing: they're just self-centered creatures who think the world revolves around them. The domme knows that this is wrong — if the world revolves around anyone, it's her. But because time thieves tend to have the skin of a rhinoceros, it can be hard to give them the message.

If it's long phone calls that are the problem, call-screen. Just because your phone rings, it doesn't mean that you have to answer it. Submissive girls jump to answer their phone, thinking that it's rude to ignore it. Nonsense. A domme knows that a phone call is simply an approach for contact. If she's not willing or able to offer her time, then she lets it ring — without feeling guilty.

If the time thief prefers the "turn up on your doorstep unexpected" approach, you just need a couple of items of clothing near the door: a hooded bathrobe and a coat. Depending on your state of (un)dress, put one of these on before you answer the door. By wearing a bathrobe, you can say "I was about to get in the bath/shower." If they still try to come in, say "I'm not alone" and calmly but firmly block their way.

And if you're wearing your coat, you can say "Oh, I was just on my way out." If your time thief tries to join you, either walk them to your nearest shop, then say "I just need to get a magazine — you go ahead. I'll see you soon" or explain that you have "forgotten" something important like your cell phone and say you have to go back to collect it but will give them a call to catch up soon.

Sometimes, passive women are complicit with time thieves. Within hours of meeting a new person they like,

Dominatricks

Always set a time limit with time wasters. If you cannot simply turn them away, be sure to explain that you have to do something in, say, half an hour. And don't feel obliged to tell them what it is. They have not earned this level of intimacy. Stay friendly, but firm, and if all else fails, crack the whip and get them out the door!

they're making foolish offers like "Call any time — I'm here for you." Strike that sentence out of your vocabulary for anyone who you know wouldn't return the favor — and anyone who you wouldn't really appreciate a phone call from at 6:00 A.M. It may sound nice but you'll only end up resenting the person concerned. Plus, a domme is good enough at making people secure in their relationship with her that anyone who deserves such an open invitation will already know that she's there for them.

And then there are work time thieves: often disorganized bosses whose lack of time-management means that you have to take the slack for them and end up working late. So book yourself a night class that starts 30 minutes after you finish work each day, and be public about your love of your horse-riding/origami/gourmet cooking course. If everyone knows that, no matter what, you have to be out of the office within 30 minutes of the end of the day — and you refuse to cancel (you can always cite non-refundable course-fees) except in times of extreme crisis — you'll teach your boss to respect that your time only belongs to them during working hours.

Just remember, you only have one life and every moment of it counts. So don't let anyone else steal something that's so precious. Your domme wouldn't allow it.

It's not always other people that are time thieves. Sometimes, the fault lies with yourself. A domme is as rigorous at dealing with her own flaws as she is with other people's, so get some time-management skills. Make a chart that has a week broken down into one-hour chunks. Every hour, write a brief description of what you've done. It may seem time consuming, but it will save you time in the long run. At the end of the week, look at the schedule and see where you're wasting time.

A common time-wasting problem is dithering, so make a vow only to touch each letter you receive once, get your e-mail inbox down to a maximum of ten e-mails each day, and never forward jokes or "virus warnings" — otherwise you're not just stealing your own time, but other people's too.

People Who Steal Attention

Attention stealing is a particularly childish form of trying to assert control over someone else's life. Most people grow out of it in their twenties but some immature and insecure people maintain the need to be the center of attention throughout their life. A domme refuses to relinquish her control that easily. She knows that everyone needs attention some of the time but that pandering to self-centered people simply isn't worth the effort because, no matter how much attention they get, they'll never be satisfied. And people who are never satisfied are no fun to be with.

Common tricks an attention stealer will use are flirting with everyone regardless of their relationship status, talking over people constantly, or wearing inappropriate clothes. (Note: This doesn't necessarily mean dressing trashy. Wearing jeans to a posh night out or an "innocent" dress to a meat market are both equally attention stealing.)

Some attention stealers will use the "constant crisis" method — something that passive women are particularly prone to responding to. This involves the attention stealer always having something wrong with their life that needs to be sorted out by someone else — namely, the submissive friend. A domme will listen, to a point, but will point out that the only person who can solve personal dilemmas is the person embroiled in them. All that anyone else can offer is advice and support, not the solution.

No matter what method attention stealers use, never try to play them at their own game. Sure, you could flirt better, wear something more attention grabbing, or have more crises — but this entails sinking to their level, and a domme has too much self-respect to play foolish games.

Instead, help the poor soul work on their self-confidence (hell, a domme is an understanding kind of woman). Let them know that you enjoy their company and think that they're fabulous but precisely because of that, you want them to work their insecurities out.

Be stern and go with the tough love thing if need be. The longer you support an attention stealer, the more this aspect of their personality will grow, and eventually they'll end up being the kind of person no one wants to be around. If it's

Whip's Words of Wisdom

Your domme wouldn't stoop to playing attention-grabbing games. She receives all the attention she needs because she is graceful and considered, witty and warm. Remember, people soon tire of moaners and bitches, but no one tires of strength and charm.

someone you value, playing tough is the only way to help. And if it's someone you don't value — well, why waste your time with them?

People Who Steal Confidence

Then there are those people who steal your confidence — or, now that you've got your inner domme, attempt to steal your confidence. You can only have your esteem knocked if you decide to pay attention to the pathetic worm who's trying to grind you down. And given that people who try to belittle others are saying more about their own insecurities than they are about you, why give them the pleasure? After all, confidence crushers are generally doing it because the only way they can see to make themselves feel better is by making other people feel worse.

Common tricks a confidence crusher will use include the backhanded compliment ("I'm so impressed you have the guts to wear a dress that tight at your size") and fake concern ("Are you sure you want to wear that?"). Another method is to raise her eyebrows and look scathing when you tell a joke or say something funny — or worse, fake a laugh.

You have various options here, apart from the obvious silent stare. Any domme knows that a bristling silence is far more uncomfortable than outright confrontation. If the behavior is constant, draw attention to it and mock it. Make sure you have a laugh in your voice, but keep fire in your eyes. If your friend only tries to steal your confidence occasionally, simply tell her she's treating you badly.

A light touch, reiterated every time the confidence crusher makes a dig, should embarrass them into treating you better, and may even help them become more aware of their behavior. Some people really don't realize that what

Dominatricks

Confidence stealers come in all shapes and sizes and, although all can be dealt with, when it comes to a parent, partner, or boss, the trick is to hold in your mind that you could cut them out of your life just like anyone else. This is a very powerful realization, and should help you to find a less extreme solution.

they're saying is hurtful and genuinely believe that they're just being honest.

But by far the most effective method is to just ignore them. Before you go out for an evening with a confidence crusher, remind yourself that she's bound to make a dig because of her personality. Have faith in your own decisions: what you wear, what you say, and how you behave. Think about it — if you were that bad, why would they want to hang out with you? And what gives them any more perspective on a situation than you have anyway?

If you still end up with your confidence in tatters at the end of an evening, after trying these tricks, there's one option left. Cut them out of your life.

Dealing with Authority

Of course, it's not always friends that try to sap your confidence or steal your time. People in authority — your boss, landlord, or an officious bureaucrat — can all make your life hell. And, let's face it, you can't call any of them a bitch. But that doesn't put a domme off. She just brings her intellectual and psychological mastery to the fore to get what she wants.

The best way to handle people in authority is to begin with the "over-sweetness" trick. It is possible to be so polite that the person feels strangely insulted. Alternatively, they may decide to treat you better because you're one of the few people who's polite to them, so it's win/win.

For example, with an officious time-stealing bureaucrat, try "I know you're terribly busy because of all of the important things that you need to do, and I'm just one of the hundreds of people that you have to deal with today, but I'd really appreciate it if you could possibly find it within yourself to help me solve this problem." (If the way the bureaucrat is stealing your time is through one of those hideous "touch three to discuss bill payments" phone systems, then just buy a speakerphone and carry on with your day-to-day tasks while you move up the queue.)

Another trick is to use flattery. A domme knows that seeming to acquiesce, while remaining in control, can be a powerful mind-game. Ask your boss if they'd mind being your mentor because you really respect them; or chat to the bureaucrat or your landlord as a "normal" person. Half the time that people behave in an authoritarian way it's because they think that they can get away with it. If they start seeing you as an equal, then their behavior will change accordingly.

"Always acknowledge a fault. This will throw those in authority off their guard and give you an opportunity to commit more."

Mark Twain
Humorist

Even if they do realize what you're doing, you can smile sweetly and say "I'm so sorry — I didn't mean you to perceive it in that way." This will probably knock their confidence too, as it introduces doubt about their own response to people. Okay, that's a bit mean, but sometimes mean works too.

Dealing with Aggression

No one should have to put up with aggression, whether physical or mental. But some people out there use it as a way to get what they want. A domme recognizes that being aggressive rather than assertive shows a lack of self-control and is basically rudeness. As such, she doesn't allow it in her life, from herself or others.

If someone is physically aggressive, and hurts you, there is only one solution: report them to the police. If you let them get away with it once, their behavior is likely to escalate. Write down a description of what happened while it's still in your mind and, if possible, get witnesses to write down an account too.

However, sometimes people can be physically aggressive without actually inflicting pain. They might invade your space or use their posture to try to make you back down in

Dominatricks

The main trick to dealing with aggression is to stay calm. That way you keep the power (something your domme has at all times). If you are treated aggressively by a stranger, be prepared to draw the line before an unknown situation gets out of hand. There's a big difference between standing firm and being foolish.

an argument. This is where your body-language tricks should come into play. Maintain your posture and keep eye contact. People often underestimate the power of the eyes but if you can unflinchingly match their gaze (no, you don't need to get into a staring match — that's just silly) while thinking "I am not threatened. I feel calm. I can cope with this," then it will show in your eyes and work on a subconscious level to make the other person back off.

It's worth bearing in mind that people are like animals — they tend to get aggressive when they're backed into a corner. As such, suggesting a "time out" alone where you

Whip's Words of Wisdom

If you feel yourself losing your temper, go into another room and punch a cushion hard or give it a few good thwacks with a spanking paddle, or if you can find somewhere sound-proofed enough, have a good scream. It's amazing how much it will relax you.

can both think about the situation without inflaming things further is a good way to counter aggression. And never chase someone who leaves a room slamming the door: if you do, they'll feel even more cornered and you can guarantee the situation will escalate.

Similarly, if it's you that starts to feel aggressive, work out the tension on your own rather than with another person. Losing your temper shows a loss of control, and automatically puts you in the losing position.

Friends Old and New

Friends have a big impact on your life — they can make you feel happy, sad, neglected, or just plain bored. Common dilemmas include friends being demanding (of your time, affection, or money), outgrowing friends but being unsure of how to move on from them, and making new friends.

If someone's demanding of your time, use the time-thieves tricks you've already learned. If they want excessive amounts of affection simply explain that you care about them but need to spend time with other people too. It may be that they're lonely and want more friends, in which case make an effort to introduce them to other people you think they'd get on with. And cash-wise, stick to the adage "Neither a borrower nor a lender be," except in extreme situations — she's stranded in town at midnight with no money to get home. And if she keeps on getting into situations and expecting you to bail her out, just stop going out together and meet at your place or hers instead. You are not responsible for your friends: that's their job — you've got your own life to manage.

A domme is honest enough with herself to admit when she's outgrown someone — and honest enough with them to tell them. However, she doesn't like causing unnecessary pain, so will do so with tact and discretion. Rather than saying "Look, we've known each other since we were kids and you've turned into a real bore nowadays," explain that you've changed and no longer have enough time to spend with as many people as you used to. As such, you're being ruthless with your time-management, and, while you really value the friendship you've had over the years, you don't feel that you can devote proper attention anymore.

If they drift away seamlessly, don't invite them back because a mixed message is worse than a harsh one. Never simply drop contact with someone (unless they've behaved

Whip Workshop
Listen Up

Whether you're dealing with a new friend or an old friend, one thing will help you maintain healthy friendships. Make sure that you listen more than you talk — it's the old "you have two ears and one mouth, use them accordingly" rule.

A domme is confident enough to know that she doesn't need to be the center of the universe (except inside her own head). As such, she is interested in other people. The more that she can find out about them, the more she adds to what she knows — whether about that person or a subject that interests them. And a domme always wants to learn more about the way that people tick.

According to research, people who do nothing other than listen and make affirmations ("Yes," "That's interesting," "Do go on") are perceived to be interesting people. Everyone loves the sound of their own voice and being allowed to fully indulge it is a rare treat.

so badly that they don't deserve your respect). It's cowardly and will leave your ex-friend over-analyzing themselves and thinking that they've done something wrong, which simply isn't fair or respectful.

As to making new friends, it's just a case of gathering up your domme confidence and being unafraid to approach people. Look for areas of common ground: if you're at a party, ask how they know the host. If you're in a coffee shop, ask about the book they're reading. Don't force yourself on them — after your initial question, smile at their response and go back to what you were doing. If they're interested in maintaining conversation, the ball's in their court. If not, carry on approaching people you think may be interesting and you'll soon find that you've got to know a lot more people.

"You can make more friends in two months by becoming interested in other people than you can in two years by trying to get other people interested in you."

Dale Carnegie
Author of How to Win Friends and Influence People

Domme and the Family

Dealing with family can be much tougher than dealing with friends. You don't get to choose your family and it's an awful lot harder to drop them if they aren't enhancing your life. However, that doesn't mean that you need to put up with bad behavior. Your domme will help you deal with things in a constructive way. To start with, she's no one's slave (quite the opposite). If your mom expects you to give her a lift to her friend's house every Saturday because you have a car, think about what's reasonable. If you have siblings, share the load. If you have a well-paid job, offer to go halves or even pay for a cab for her. That way, you're still being supportive but aren't letting her run your life.

The festive season can bring out particularly unpleasant or demanding behavior from your family. There may be an expectation that you'll spend every Thanksgiving together. Nip it in the bud and warn people early: for example, say at Thanksgiving dinner "This is lovely. I'm going to miss it next year when I'm in Barbados/at my boyfriend's house/at the yoga retreat." That way, you're softening the blow and giving your family time to adjust. If you haven't got time to do that — Thanksgiving is around the corner and you'd rather pull out your own toenails than endure another day of squabbling — plead work or say that you're helping out at a soup kitchen, as both of these things are less likely to start a row.

It can also be useful to cave on things that aren't that important to you — say, changing a lightbulb for your grandma because she can't reach it, even if it does mean a bit of an inconvenient trip. That way, you've got the moral high ground and can't have the line "You never do anything for your family" thrown at you when you refuse to do something that you really don't want to do.

Oh, and if you slide into "adolescent mode" every time you go to see your family, get a grip. Limit the amount of time that you spend with them to an hour, two hours, or however long you can cope without punching the walls — having told your family that you can only stay for that amount of time — and be firm about adhering to your boundaries. Make sure that you leave after the time period specified even if you're having a nice time. This way you will avoid the "but last time you stayed longer" comment the next time you go to visit and are seething within minutes.

Whip Workshop
Sibling Sense

When it comes to siblings, a little bit of understanding of the impact of birth order can make it much easier to understand unacceptable behavior.

Generally speaking, eldest children feel that power is their right. They can be strict, bossy, or helpful (which can be a good thing but can make their siblings feel controlled).

Middle children tend to be even-tempered but may struggle to find their place in the world because they feel "sandwiched" between their siblings.

Youngest children are frequently spoiled, want to be more important (bigger) than their siblings, and often have grand plans that never work out.

By understanding that these characteristics are a product of birth position, it can be easier to overlook them because it means your sibling isn't being deliberately obstructive. However, let them know the impact of birth order too, as it will help them work it through — and show them where your negatives come from too.

By far the hardest family to deal with is your own, once you have kids. After all, you can't just walk out on them if they annoy you. Instead, set boundaries (having a "naughty step" to send children to — one minute for every year of their life — when they misbehave will give you a useful time-out and, because children don't like being ignored, should help them behave better). And if they're adolescent, sorry, you're just going to have to accept they'll be a nightmare for a few years. Even a domme balks slightly facing a roomful of adolescents. Just remember, it will pass.

Partner Domme-style

And then there's the major player: your partner. You've chosen to spend your time/life with them, love is probably involved and your body is awash with chemicals that have an impact on your behavior.

Common problems in a long-term relationship include one or both partners taking each other for granted, one person falling into the role of housekeeper/adult while the other takes the junior role, and money issues. A good way to see whether you're being taken for granted — or are being overly demanding of your partner — is to imagine for a second that you're friends instead. Would you feel comfortable with the way you're being treated or the way that you treat your partner if they were a friend? If not, moderate your behavior accordingly. All too often people speak less politely to their partner than they would to a stranger or simple acquaintance.

If you end up doing all the housework — the average woman does 3,000 hours of unpaid housework a year — stop right now. You may panic that the house will get into a state but there are solutions. Clean with your partner rather than alone — it can almost become fun if you do it together. And they're more likely to help you with the dishes if you turn it into something fun (say, by wearing stockings — a domme knows how to use her sexuality to her advantage). Alternatively, make a deal between you, splitting the jobs. If both of you say the job that you most hate, then you can make it less arduous by doing the job that they hate most and vice versa (if it's the same chore, take it in turns). Or, if you can afford it, just get a cleaner and spend the time you would have spent cleaning on a date instead.

And then there are financial problems. All too often, one person in a couple is good with money while the other fritters it away. Whatever you do, avoid getting a joint bank account that has all your money in it. It just leads to trouble and is archaic in today's world anyway. Set up an account for bills, and both set up standing orders to transfer the right amount of money into the account each month. If the bills are covered, what does it matter if you spend your spare money on shoes or your partner spends theirs on DVDs?

You — Your Own Worst Enemy

Once you've sorted out your friends, family, and partner, there's still one person you need to fix though: yourself. Yes, I know we've done this, but how you let yourself react to others is a major part of taking control of them. Too many women let self-doubt afflict their life. A domme won't stand for any of that nonsense.

If you do something wrong, apologize immediately if it damaged someone else or forgive yourself for being flawed if it only affected you. Everyone makes mistakes and despite the perfection culture we live in, you can guarantee that even the person you most admire has probably done something similar at some stage in their life.

You also need to accept that you won't be a nice person all the time. Sure, it'd be great if we always thought of other people and behaved in an exemplary fashion — but we're human. Think of all the nasty urges that you hold back to put your behavior into perspective. If you find yourself immersed in self-doubt on a regular basis, consider getting counseling to work things through. There are probably reasons for your behavior, but this doesn't mean that you should use them as an excuse. That's weak and pathetic — something a domme refuses to be. Once you know the root, it's easier to move on to being a happier you.

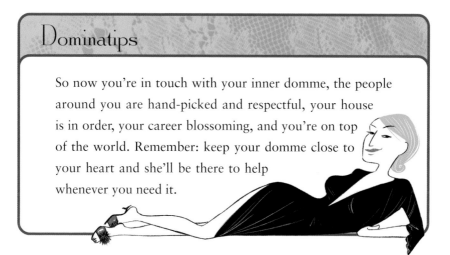

Dominatips

So now you're in touch with your inner domme, the people around you are hand-picked and respectful, your house is in order, your career blossoming, and you're on top of the world. Remember: keep your domme close to your heart and she'll be there to help whenever you need it.

Taking control of love

A domme knows that she deserves a perfect partner. Her bare minimum requirements are trust, respect, and affection. If her partner provides all three, they're in for some red hot passion. If not, they're out the door.

Dating with Your Domme

Many women often bemoan the lack of decent singles in the world, worry that they'll end up alone, and say "yes" to anyone that asks them out. A domme knows what she wants and goes out to get it. She realizes that there are thousands of people out there who'd adore her: but she's only going to commit to one who's perfect.

Think about the people you've been out with. Have they treated you with respect? Turned up to dates on time, called you back when you've left them a message, and clearly been proud to have you on their arm? If so, good, it's what you deserve and I trust you treat them the same way. If not, it's time to let your domme shine through.

Like it or not, people only treat you badly if they think that they can get away with it. So make it obvious that you won't put up with it. If someone's frequently late for a date without calling you to explain and apologize, call a friend and go out with them instead. If a partner never calls you back, stop calling them. It's amazing how attentive someone will get if they feel you slipping away from them. And if someone's clearly ashamed to be with you and won't

Domme's Dos & Don'ts — Choosing a Lover

What's it about?

✓ It's about finding someone who is respectful of all women and would not make negative comments about other women to woo you.

✓ It's about avoiding other people's baggage, especially if they have it out on show.

✓ It's about finding someone who is self-aware and generous, but still has a glint in their eye.

✓ It's about finding someone who controls their vices rather than being controlled by them.

✓ It's about finding someone who is single and free to adore you — and who you can adore in return.

What's it not about?

✖ It's not about accepting someone who talks about their ex or makes you feel anything less than wonderful.

✖ It's not about accepting someone just because they're available, but who makes your stomach turn.

✖ It's not about accepting someone who is self-deluded or who believes that you are in any way inferior.

✖ It's not about taking on someone else's needs, inferiorities, drink or drug problems. You're not their mother.

✖ It's not about taking on someone who is attached. There are enough hurdles for women in the world without us setting up more for each other.

introduce you to their friends (within a reasonable time period, not on date one), then ditch them. Life's too short to waste on people who get your confidence down.

A domme has faith in herself. As such, she eschews game-playing — say, refusing to put out for the first three dates, waiting 48 hours before returning a phone call for fear of looking too keen, or flirting with someone else to arouse jealousy. A domme knows the importance of honesty and demands it in herself as much as in others. And she doesn't let other people get away with game-playing either: sulking to get their own way, or flirting with someone else,

Whip's Words of Wisdom

A domme believes in making a swift and positive recovery from rejection of any kind and does not taking being dumped to heart. A domme would never chase after someone who has rejected her and would never let herself be unable to "get over" it. A true domme gets back up and gets back out there.

or ignoring her and expecting her to come running. Instead, she is utterly herself and expects the same from her partner.

If she feels horny, she'll seduce her partner (assuming that they're happy about it — she'll never push someone's boundaries). If she feels neglected, she'll either tell her partner and ask them to sort it out, will seek attention from friends, or will boost her own confidence by doing something she loves. And if someone makes her feel bad about herself, she leaves them.

The domme is a romantic. She believes in love, and respects it. She knows that love is a magical thing between the right people and can't be forced. As a result, she won't mess with people's emotions: if someone's in love with her and she doesn't feel the same way, she'll tell them. If she falls for someone who's not into her, she'll back off as soon as this is clear. But she'll do everything in her power to nurture real love, if and when it appears.

Domme-seeking Missile

A domme would rather be single than settle for anything less than the best but she also wants a great sex life. That doesn't necessarily mean swinging from the rafters: everyone has

"Love is everything it's cracked up to be. It really is worth fighting for, being brave for, risking everything for."

Erica Jong
Award-winning poet, novelist, and essayist

different libido levels, so she wants someone who meets her standards and who has a similar sex drive to her own. Few things are worse than having to nag someone in order to get any action — or having to constantly turn them down because they want it more than you do.

To find your match, start by making a list of all your desired traits — and any top turnoffs. Be precise — for example, rather than "likes pop music" put "knows all the words to *Dirty* by Christina Aguilera." Read it every day to imprint it in your mind and you'll start to attract people who fit the bill (really, this works — it's using a psychological technique called Positive Visualization).

And don't be afraid to approach people you fancy, even (especially) if you think they're out of your league. Men aren't used to being approached and they'll admire your courage. Passive girls may balk at approaching men but a domme has a mantra that helps her maintain her attitude. "If I talk to him, I've got a 50 percent chance of success. If I don't, I've got 100 percent chance of failure." Have a glass of wine to boost your confidence by all means but don't get drunk — you won't come across well.

In the everyday world, a woman with her confidence intact rarely has to resort to using her body to get what she wants, but in a love situation, it's time to flash the flesh! Make sure you're comfortable and in control with what you're

Whip's Words of Wisdom

Listen more than you talk, as research shows that he'll think that you have a lot in common, particularly if you smile and nod at what he's saying. Use all the body language tricks you've learned and make light physical contact — brush his arm or tap his knee when one of you makes a joke.

doing, and that your actions won't get you into trouble. "If you're wearing a skirt, touch your leg to draw attention to it. Caress your collarbone and run your finger down to your cleavage," suggests Sarah Hedley, editor of British sex magazine, *Scarlet*.

If it's getting to the end of the night and he doesn't look like he'll be making the first move, it's time to be bold — even brazen. If you want a relationship, say to him "I've really enjoyed chatting with you — fancy doing it again some time?" If he is keen, arrange another meeting, perhaps somewhere more intimate.

Dominatricks

Use an excuse to get him to talk to you. Drop something of yours in front of him or ask him for directions. Change your body language and see if he copies it. Be friendly. Maintain eye contact and smile. It'll make you appear easygoing and approachable. Speak quietly so he has to lean closer to you. Say things that are meant for his ears only.

Whip Workshop
Distance Dating

Still nervous about approaching men in person? Then join a dating website. Nowadays, there are dating sites for every type of person; artistic people, gorgeous people, every racial group, vegetarians — the list is endless. Most include some form of safety mechanism so that you can talk to someone online without having to divulge your real e-mail address or other contact details.

Dating sites give you a chance to get to know someone before you go out with them, and are also great for reminding you how many singles there are out there. Some even include an option to add people to your "favorites," which is a subtle way of expressing interest as they can see that you've listed them as a favorite and initiate contact if they're interested too (it's also a great ego boost seeing who's listed you in their favorites).

But hell, why be so shy — with your domme attitude, you should have the guts to contact whoever you like the look of. With a flick of the wrist and a click of the mouse, you could find someone that you truly click with.

When you are together, particularly at his home or yours, remember the rules about confident communication from Chapter 1. Sitting opposite him at a table just introduces an unnecessary barrier and will make it harder for him to make a move (remember, men get shy too). Sit still and be calm, jumping up and down to make coffee will put up barriers and make him as uncomfortable as you.

In your own home, you need to make sure that your rooms are in a fit state for visitors — but a domme is always in control so you'll already have this one covered. It should go without saying that your home should be tidy and clean. But that's only one tiny part of scene setting.

Get some incense, scented candles, or fresh flowers so that your home smells sweet. Remove any self-help manuals (including this one) from view — you don't want him to think that you need advice. He should feel that you're just a wise and worldly woman. And make sure that you don't have any pictures of exes visible — it will suggest you're not over them, and be sure to put him off his stroke.

Cuddly toys on the bed are another no-no — they suggest you're trying to cling on to your childhood (one battered old teddy bear is acceptable — just — but only if it's perched on the end of the bed, not tucked in).

Whatever the setting, make the space your own. Don't be overly anxious about your words or actions; after all, he's chosen to spend time with you so make sure he sees you at your best, and give him a chance to be at his best too. That way you'll both enjoy the experience.

The Domme in Love

After the heady days of dating, chances are you'll have found a man who fulfills your every need — after all, you've got your domme on your side and she'll never settle for less than great.

If you and your man are moving toward the longer-term relationship, then there is already love in the air, but there also needs to be some practical consideration. Remember your boundaries. The boundaries you set at the beginning will help to shape every part of your relationship, from romantic gestures to time keeping. You both need to decide how much time and space you want to give to the relationship — be this 24-7 or a more leisurely pace. If you feel that either of you is investing much more or much less than the other, address the issue. The surest way to undo the

"I don't need a man. But I'm happier with one. I like to have someone I can touch and squeeze and kiss. But I don't fold up and die if I don't have a man around."

Cher
Singer and actress

passion is for one partner to feel that they are doing all the running. Once you both feel that there is an equal interest and investment you can concentrate on making the time you spend together that much more special.

If you feel ready to take the relationship to the next stage, make sure that the timing and setting are right for you. In every aspect of your life, not just in the bedroom, it's important that you don't allow anyone to pressure you into any actions you don't feel fully comfortable with. And if they try, don't be afraid to walk away.

Whatever the stage of your relationship, the only reason to have sex with someone is because you want to and just because you've dated, kissed, or even indulged in foreplay, it doesn't mean that you owe your man anything. Nonetheless it's best to set ground rules before you start so that there's no awkwardness. If you're honest there should be no problem.

If you are interested in having sex with your man, before anything else you need to tackle the safe sex question. This should hold no embarrassment for either of you. It is more important to establish safety than be concerned about nerves, shyness, tact, or what your man might or might not think of you. In fact, it's less of a question and more of a demand because the only answer you should accept when

Whip's Words of Wisdom

Respect and honesty lie at the heart of any truly loving relationship. Your man is not a mind-reader. You have to take responsibility for letting him know what you feel and what you need, otherwise the gap between what he does and what you want him to do might drive your relationship apart.

asking someone to take precautions is "Yes." If a man refuses, show him the door because he doesn't respect you, and a domme doesn't deal with someone who lacks respect for her and her needs.

If you or your man has had sexual partners before, ensure that you get tested for all STDs (sexually transmitted diseases) before you consider unprotected sex. Otherwise you're literally risking your life.

Remember, sex is about mutual pleasure so don't just lie there. Take charge. Remember, there's nothing wrong with asking for what you want in the bedroom — a domme is unashamed of her sexuality. So if you want to try something different, just say. If your partner declines, don't insist — after all, good sex is about mutual respect.

If it turns out you're sexually incompatible, don't be afraid to address the problem. Sex is an important part of a relationship for a lot of people, so if you're not having fun (despite showing him what you like) you're clearly not suited as lovers.

If all is working well and you know what you enjoy sexually, tell your partner. And, even if you have been together for a while, it never hurts to turn up the passion and try something new.

Women who are confident in the bedroom know that any spoken sexual request that starts with a compliment will encourage her man to respond. It will also encourage him to talk openly about what he likes. This means you can both take greater pleasure in the physical side of your relationship. Always listen to your partner's desires but don't ever feel pressured into acting on them if they make you uncomfortable or unsure.

Making changes in the bedroom can work wonders on an established relationship that has become routine. You don't need to change everything overnight, but by opening

Dominatricks

A domme knows what she wants because she's thoroughly explored her own body and feels comfortable with it. One of the greatest tricks to having fun in the bedroom is to leave all sense of nervousness about your body image outside the door — your body is perfect for you and for your man — and he knows it.

avenues of communication and enjoying your lovemaking, both you and your partner will feel refreshed with one another and should be able to talk more effectively about other elements of your relationship.

Taking Charge

Of course, it's not just in the bedroom that a domme will assert herself. She expects all aspects of her relationship to be right. That doesn't mean perfect — there is no such thing

Dominatricks

A domme knows that real confidence is as much about saying "no" as saying "yes." If your man's behavior doesn't come up to scratch, there are always punishments you can mete out. Similarly, the rewards for good behavior should be at hand for whenever there's a special treat to be had.

as perfection so aiming for it will just leave you feeling disappointed. But a relationship should be evenly balanced, honest, and fun. If not, why waste your valuable time?

Common things men do that annoy women include refusing to talk about the relationship, being less affectionate than the woman, or being a slob. All of these can be easily dealt with.

In the first case, think about why you need to talk about the relationship. Knowing where you stand is obviously important but if you need to constantly analyze the relationship, you're showing insecurity — and a domme isn't insecure. Generally, the only reason to talk about the relationship is if you're falling in love — or there are relationship problems.

If you start to have strong feelings for someone, be emotionally brave and admit it, though never the first time you feel it — give yourself at least three more dates before you commit yourself to any declarations. (It's much harder taking back an "I love you" than saying it in the first place.)

Rather than asking "Where do you see this relationship going?" say that you're beginning to think you could fall for the guy concerned and ask whether he thinks it's a good idea. Take note, never say love at this stage — it's a scary word for lots of men and the aim here is to test the water in a non-threatening way. This gives him the scope to tell you to back off — which you should react to calmly — or confess his feelings and you can act accordingly.

Never think you can convince someone to fall in love with you. If they don't have the same feeling as you, they can't switch it on, no matter how wonderfully you treat them nor how long you persevere.

If there are problems in the relationship, state them clearly and without blame — rather than "You always ignore me when you're with your friends," say, "I feel a bit neglected when you talk to your friends and not me." That way, he has information to act on and you're more likely to get an apology too. It may be he didn't even realize he was upsetting you.

"The reason husbands and wives do not understand each other is because they belong to different sexes."

Dorothea Dix
Philanthropist and social reformer

Whip Workshop
Moving On

After a relationship ends, you'll probably feel down (even if you're the person that ended it). So allocate time to cheering yourself up. It's fine to do the cathartic "watching a soppy film, eating ice-cream and sobbing" thing after the initial breakup — but don't wallow in it.

Instead, head out with your best girlfriends, treat yourself. Avoid a make-over, however. The freshly single are in no fit state of mind to pick a new look (and you'll probably end up with a hideous haircut). Get some exercise that you enjoy to get those happy endorphins flowing again. Keeping busy will keep your mind off what you would be doing if you were still with . . . what's his name again?

Don't get tempted to go with the adage "The only way to get over a man is to get under another." It will end in rebound tears. Well, not unless he's really cute anyway.

Remember, a domme doesn't need a man to feel on top of the world.

When a guy's less affectionate than you'd like, tell him that kisses/hugs/whatever other affection you crave makes you feel horny. He'll change his behavior pretty sharpish.

Slobs come in many forms. Some are well turned out, but live in filth. Others seem mortally afraid of soap and water. For the former, simply refuse to enter his home until he shows you the respect you deserve and makes the place comfortable for you. Offer help if he needs it, but never, never clean up after him. For the latter, use some more cunning tactics. Start a date with a sexy shower, then tell him how gorgeous he smells and how much that makes you want to get closer to him. It's easier to train a man using positive reinforcement than nagging — back to those domme mind-games again.

If your man refuses to clean up his act, explain that you don't find this sexy. If it comes to a choice between being a slob and being with you, only a real loser would choose the former, and a domme does not allow losers into her realm.

And if after all your efforts he still hasn't responded, there's only one thing for it. Get the loser out of your life and find someone who behaves properly. You don't have time to waste on someone who doesn't willingly add to your happiness or pleasure.

And If It Ends . . .

Passive girls cling on to relationships that are way past their sell-by date because they're scared of being alone. A domme enjoys her own company so isn't afraid to break away from someone who isn't making her happy.

If a relationship starts to feel unpleasant in the early days, she gets out rather than trying to work things through, not because she's afraid of commitment but because she knows the first three months of a relationship are the headiest due to the chemicals that are produced by the body when you first meet someone you fancy. As such, if things are bad in the early days despite the chemicals, there's no future for the relationship (other than a bad one).

If it's a longer-term thing, you may be tempted to try to make it work so you haven't "thrown away five years" (or however long you were together). However, if you think about it, the longer you stay in a bad relationship, the more of your life you're wasting.

It takes guts to split with someone — particularly if part of you still cares about them — but you've got those guts now. So explain that things aren't working and need to end.

Don't use it as an excuse to go over old arguments though. You're moving on, and don't want to make the guy feel any worse than he already does at losing a prize like you. Hold your ground no matter how much your partner grovels or cries. It's your life that you're wasting otherwise.

If a guy is making you feel anything less than fantastic, he simply doesn't deserve you and you don't deserve to be giving him the time of day. "The powerful woman always calls up her confidence and ends any relationship, be it professional or personal, with calm and self-control," says psychologist Dr. Lisa Matthewman. But rather than writing a letter or sending a text message, you should tell it like it is, face to face if possible. Dr Lisa continues, "You should never be unkind or disrespectful whatever the circumstances. You should simply say, 'You know, I deserve to be in a relationship where we're both happy and we're both getting what we deserve . . . and this isn't it.'"

In the end, it is your responsibility to make sure you are happy in your relationship. Your domme will help you address the problems with an honest appraisal. If your partner refuses to accept the points you raise or the needs you voice, then there is really no option but to firmly close the door for good.

Domme Stands Alone

So, now your love life should be perfectly whipped into shape. Your partner is attentive, honest, loving, and loyal. He calls to let you know where he is, he arrives with flowers, surprise trips away, and loves nothing more than to sit and rub your feet. No? Well, don't beat yourself up. Your inner domme may take a while to develop: after all, she's all about building your confidence and that doesn't happen overnight. Pay attention to her and feel proud every time your domme rises up and comes to the fore.

Dominatips

When you deal with the people around you remember that they should be giving as well as receiving. Don't allow anyone to force a one-sided relationship on you. The next step is to whip into shape the major areas of your life — time, money, home, and work.

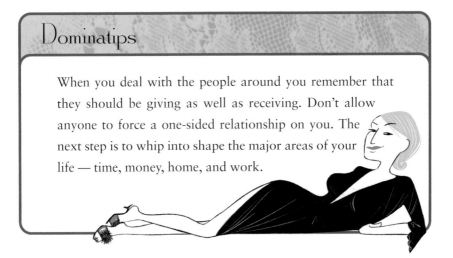

Taking control
of your life

Now that you've whipped the people in your life into shape, it's time to deal with your life itself. This may seem like a huge undertaking, but a domme handles things with precision in order to maintain control. She knows that by paying close attention, and breaking things down into their individual elements, they become manageable.

Balancing It All

By far the biggest problem most people have in their lives is fitting in everything that they want to do. Work/life balance is getting more off-kilter with every year that passes. And merely calling it work/life balance oversimplifies matters ridiculously. The "life" aspect includes fitting in friendships, family, and relationships; managing your money; keeping your home in a good state; and generally maintaining a feeling of well-being.

But it's entirely possible to fit all of these things into your life, with a bit of time-management. And a domme loves time-management because it's about taking control of every second.

Use traveling time to read, catch up on work, paint your nails, or practice yogic breathing exercises. If you're waiting for someone in a work situation, text a friend to organize your evening's entertainment. When you're sitting in a bar and your friend goes to the toilet, use the spare few minutes to place a call you need to make. And if you have a meeting that's near a friend who you don't get to see much, try to arrange it for the end of the day so that you can meet them afterward.

Domme's Dos & Don'ts – Life Management

What's it about?

✔ It's about taking stock of the elements of your life that hold you back, from paying bills to having a career. Then taking back control.

✔ It's about managing your time and making sure that you don't waste a second on unnecessary tasks.

✔ It's about controlling your money rather than it controlling you.

✔ It's about keeping the running of your home easy and manageable and attacking each project with a view to releasing time for yourself.

✔ It's about being in charge at work. In charge of your time, of your job, of your colleagues, and of your future.

What's it not about?

✘ It's not about ignoring your responsibilities and letting your life pile up around you as if you don't care about it.

✘ It's not about doing less in your life in order to cope with the demands life throws at you.

✘ It's not about doing without, taking endless credit, or hiding from your bank manager.

✘ It's not about frenzied cleaning or not letting friends relax in your home.

✘ It's not about being bossy with colleagues or ignoring the needs of your job.

"Time is the coin of your life. It is the only coin you have, and only you can determine how it will be spent. Be careful lest you let other people spend it for you."

Carl Sandburg
Poet

If you feel like you never get everything you need to do fitted into your life, make a list at the start of every week, divided into columns: Work, Friends, Household, etc. Then write down the tasks you need to do, be that attending a meeting, going for a drink with a pal, or paying your gas bill. Tick each thing off as you do it. That way, you'll see that you're making progress and will be able to maintain motivation and see what free time you have.

And remember the "no" lesson. Don't be scared to say that you won't be able to do something, whether that's going out with a work colleague socially when you don't really enjoy their company, or doing the laundry for a couple of days. That said, remember, if you do household chores as you go along, they take a lot less time: rather than having a cup of tea and then putting it in the sink, just rinse it out and use the same cup the next time you have tea. Washing plates as soon as you finish eating takes less time than washing a plate with congealed food. And putting your clothes straight into the washing machine when you take them off saves you minutes of picking clothes up.

It's also worth working out your most efficient time of day. This varies from person to person, but if you save your most challenging tasks for your most efficient time, they'll get done a lot quicker (and it'll mean that you can spend your downtime doing the easy jobs).

Dominatricks

At work, only touch each piece of paper once — then either file it, respond to it, or pitch it. Limit unnecessary emails: use one phone call if it would take ten emails to do the same job. And try to keep gossip to a minimum. It may seem like a fun way to spend the day but it's less fun when you're still working into the night.

Money Matters

No matter how much of a domme you are, you're not going to be able to get out of paying the rent — well, not unless you have a pretty domme relationship with your landlord. And even if you're lucky enough to be in that situation, the same trick isn't going to work on the utilities companies. So, you need to whip your bank balance into shape.

You might be lucky and never get the fear when your bank statement pops through your door. But most people, at some stage in their life, have had panic kick in after a heavy shopping spree (well, a domme needs to keep herself in shiny boots). Don't stress. Something dommes know is that fear can be controlled — and even used to your advantage. After all, if you become terrified that you're about to have your car repossessed because you haven't paid your loan off, then you're a lot more likely to want to do something about it.

Similarly, far too many people are scared of approaching a cash machine, or at the very least will refuse to check their balance and try to escape the scene as soon as possible. The domme scorns such behavior. Instead, get to know your bank balance. The better you know something (or someone)

Whip Workshop
Where Your Money Goes

If you're lousy with money, you probably don't even know where it goes. So, call for back-up. A domme always has people on her side to help out when things get tricky or she needs a helping hand.

Ask your friends what they think you spend your money on. They may spot things you don't. Whether it's take-out meals, drink, or clothes. Once you know what your weaknesses are, you can deal with them.

Keep your receipts. File them, then at the end of each week (yes, each week — you want to stay on top all the time) work out how much you've spent, and what you've spent it on, so you can spot any room for improvement.

And calculate how much disposable income you have once you've paid your monthly bills. Take that cash out of the bank and use it to fund your dalliances. When it runs out, you'll know that you're done. Then you can do something about it, be that getting a second job, cutting back, or finding cheaper alternatives for a while.

the more room you've got for making it do what you want. And it also means that you know when to do a friend a favor, so you can extort a free meal out of them in return. Make sure that you're the one who's controlling your money, rather than the other way around, and your bank balance will happily change from red to black.

And if you checked your bank balance and it's a little on the "blushing" side? Before you read the next sentence get your domme ready. OK, you're feisty, fearless, and ready for anything? Cool. So, go to see your bank manager — or at the very least, give them a call. If you're broke, they'll be able to help you sort out a loan — or a repayment scheme that you can afford. Even if you're loaded, you should call them: then they'll help you get the most out of your money.

Wimps cower every time a bill drops through the door. A domme faces up to her responsibilities, knowing that with a little work, anything can be taken in hand and thoroughly sorted out. So stop fretting, see your bank manager, and follow their advice. It's not relinquishing control — it's handing it over to someone who knows more than you do.

Then, be stern with yourself. Work out how much you can afford to spend, take that amount of cash out each week, and leave home without your ATM card. Forgo expensive take-out coffee on the way into the office and take your own in with you. Sell clothes you've grown out of or got bored with to your friends or a designer shop. And use your brain. Deep down, you know what it is that's taking your cash. So cut it out of your life and find an alternative.

If you manage your money there's always a chance for a reward each month — but remember to punish yourself if you fail to do what you're told. It's the domme's way of ensuring you stick to the rules.

Whip's Words of Wisdom

As with everything else, a domme controls her money. Even if you know that the essentials are covered, remember that there's always the element of the unexpected — be it a flat tire or an invitation away — so keep a little aside. Don't let your finances be the ultimate dictator in your life.

Clearing the Decks

It's all too easy to get into bad habits, socially, at work, or when it comes to household management. It can seem like an uphill struggle simply getting through the commitments you've made each week. But that's not going to happen anymore. A domme refuses to struggle (though she will fight for what she wants). She simply gets her life back on track by re-setting her boundaries. And the best way to do that is by clearing the decks.

The aim here is to get rid of anything that you no longer need in your life: friends, conflicts at home and work, belongings — it's all up for grabs.

"Sometimes the greatest gain in productive energy will come from cleaning the cobwebs, dealing with old business, and clearing the decks."

David Allen
Author of *Getting Things Done*

Start with the conflicts as these can take up the most time: every hour you spend stewing about a row you've had is an hour wasted. So, either apologize or move on from the person you've got the conflict with. Obviously, this is easier if it's a partner or friend, but if your boss or a family member is making your life hell, don't think that you have to put up with it. You can change jobs. And while it's not ideal, you can drop contact with a family member too if they're a negative influence on your life. The main reason that people cling on to old situations rather than resolving them is fear: of being wrong or of losing someone. A domme isn't scared of tackling things head-on, regardless of the consequences, as long as her decisions are considered, not impetuous moves.

Next, look over your time-management chart and see how you spend the bulk of your time. Is there anything you waste time on that can be eliminated from your life: a hobby you've outgrown, or a habit like watching TV? Do you spend hours every week cooking for yourself, when you could get ready meals or spend a few hours on a Sunday cooking all your food for the week then putting it in the freezer so you only have a few minutes of defrosting to do when you get home from work? Do you get up early to go to the gym before work, when walking to work each day would keep you just as fit but get you a bit more time in bed and save you money? Or do you waste half the weekend sleeping or lazing around? Clear all your bad habits from your life and you'll find you have more time.

Then, look at your belongings. If you have a wardrobe, shoes and all, that would put Imelda Marcos to shame, think about whether you really need all those clothes. The more you have to choose from, the longer you'll take to get ready every day. Try to hone it down into a capsule wardrobe, so that almost any two items that you pull out will go with each

Dominatricks

Clutter is not only a factor of space and time. Emotional clutter can be equally oppressive and demoralizing. If you have an old argument that is still unresolved or are feeling angry or frustrated by someone but have not addressed it, you must make the decision to face it or to let it go. Pick up the whip and clear the air. Either way the clutter must be cleared.

other. If you're a shopping queen, don't panic — you can always use accessories to liven an outfit up (but again, make sure they coordinate with all your outfits to save time).

Once you've cleared the decks socially, professionally, and cleared out your wardrobe, it's time to move onto the biggest clear-out. Your home.

Domme-estic Bliss

Look at your everyday life and decide how to make the best of your time. If you have a partner, are the responsibilities regarding chores and children shared equally between you? Do you both spend sufficient time with each other, the kids, and all together as a family? If you live alone, do you waste time avoiding chores rather than getting them out of the way? Spend half an hour drawing out a "home-life" timetable for your week. For the housework allocate yourselves an allotted time for each job, and stick to it. Look at the hectic areas — if you struggle with morning routines, plan what you can do the night before to ease the load. You'll get stuff done without a rush so you won't scream at the kids, you won't be screamed at by your boss, and less stress will mean you won't feel as tired. By feeling in control of your life you'll feel better prepared to address any situation, from learning a language, paying your bills, or bringing up your kids, with positivity and power.

Housework is a necessary evil — but unless you live alone, there's no reason that it should be entirely your burden. Sharing labor equally is one of the main advantages of sharing a place, after all.

The domme always sets the ground rules before doing anything, so make sure that you've got yours in place before you move in with someone, whether a stranger, friend, or lover. Be honest about your bad habits and ask them to do the same. That way, you're prepared — and can work out compromises before you both get irritated beyond all belief and the relationship falters over who does the dishes.

"They say that time changes things, but you actually have to change them yourself."

Andy Warhol
Artist

Whip Workshop
Keeping Order

Don't just think filing is for the office. It can make your life run much more smoothly at home too. Get a series of files. Into one of them, put all the take-out menus that you have. Use another one for all bills (for your records only: ideally, you should set up direct debits for all your bills so you don't have to waste time by paying them manually). Put any tradespeople's cards into a third folder (cleaners, boiler repair people, painters, and decorators). And put any communal membership cards — e.g., video club memberships — into another file.

Set up as many files as you need to run your life: one could have spare keys, another could have recipes — whatever you need to make your life run more smoothly.

Keep the folders in the same place and make sure everyone knows where it is. That way, whenever you need something it will be easily accessible.

If you already live with someone and the place has descended into chaos, agree that you'll both do a mass clear-out together and then keep things tidy from that point. By setting aside a weekend to have a thorough clear out, you'll have less stuff to tidy up from that day forward.

Have two sets of refuse sacks, ideally in different colors. In one of them, put any rubbish (if you're keeping something because it might be useful, but you haven't used it in a year, throw it away). In the other, put anything that's saleable/suitable to go to a charity shop. Don't throw away anything that belongs to anyone else — just put it in a pile for them to go through.

If you have kids, get them involved too, with their own bags. By turning it into a game — who can tidy their room the fastest — they'll be more likely to join in.

Establishing routines is another good way to keep your household running smoothly: every time you move from one room to another, take something with you that needs moving there. When you finish eating, put the dishes next to the sink or in the dishwasher. When you have a bath, rinse the tub out immediately. Open and deal with mail each morning. Little and often will make running your household much less of a chore.

The Domme at Work

It's not just at home that domme skills come in handy. They can also help you at work. After all, a domme always achieves the result she wants, which obviously has a massive impact on your career. A submissive woman will stay in a job she hates because she's scared of leaving something secure. But a domme has the guts to go for her dream, be that following a vocation, earning enough money to retire at 40 and spend the rest of her life relaxing, or a series of part-time jobs that leave her free to travel the world or spend her time on hobbies that she enjoys.

The first step is to work out what it is that you really want to do. Think of the time in your life when you were happiest and that should give you an idea of where your priorities lie. Maybe it was when you were working on your student newspaper: so follow that journalism dream. Or perhaps it was when you were traveling and didn't have a care in the world. So go back to traveling and take bar jobs to support yourself. No matter what your dream entails — be it housewife or hedonist — if you commit yourself wholeheartedly to achieving it, it will happen.

Once you've spent time thinking about what you want, you might decide that you've got your dream job already. But if you're in a job that doesn't suit you, scour the jobs pages (not forgetting the many job sites online) and find something else that will. Don't let people know that you're looking; you should be in control of when you leave a job — a domme doesn't get sacked for lack of commitment. If you don't have a computer at home, borrow a friend's or use a public one in a library or Internet café to write your CV rather than using the computer at work.

When looking for a job, aim high and go for what you really want rather than settling for something less. After all, we spend half our waking hours at work so it's a large chunk of your life you're wasting if you don't do something you enjoy and that gives you a sense of achievement.

Whether you're happy in your job or not, you should respect it, and be utterly committed to it, no matter how menial it may seem. Commitment doesn't mean that you should work unpaid overtime or become a workaholic — that's the kind of nonsense passive girls put up with. But you should treat colleagues with respect, deliver at least as much as your boss wants, and behave professionally in the workplace at all times.

Whip Workshop
Network, Network, Network

If you want to succeed professionally, you need to network. Every time you're out, it's a networking opportunity. A domme isn't scared of initiating contact with new people — or being a shameless self-publicist. She knows that, as long as she gives as much attention to other people as she generates for herself, she'll earn respect.

If you meet someone interesting, even if they're not immediately relevant to your job, get their phone number and arrange to meet them again. Once you have a circle of interesting people around you, you can introduce them to each other. And after you've introduced them to each other, they'll feel that they owe you a favor and will introduce you to more interesting people. Before long, you'll be the hub of a dynamic group of people — the person who knows everyone.

A domme never gives away her secrets so when someone asks how you know so many people, just smile sweetly and say you just "like people."

Most importantly, if you want your boss to respect you, make sure that you "manage upward." This involves controlling and manipulating your boss's expectations — under-promise and over-deliver and you'll be perceived as a shining star.

You should also be honest about any issues that you have at work — without whining. If your boss asks you to do something that's unfeasible, don't just say "yes" and panic. Explain that you don't think it will be possible and give the reasons why. And then — this is the essential bit — suggest an alternative. A boss wants solutions, not problems, so if

Dominatricks

Always dress as if you've got an important meeting. You never know when one will crop up and if you're constantly prepared, then you'll attract your boss's attention in a good way. Try to make the most of your time, even when you go to make a coffee or have a cigarette. Take memos to read or any papers to deliver on the way. That way, you'll not be wasting a moment.

Domme's Dos & Don'ts — Making Work Work for You

What's it about?

✓ It's about assessing your working life and ensuring that you're moving forward all the time.

✓ It's about tackling problems with your boss, workload, or colleagues in a practical, positive way.

✓ It's about planning your own career path and taking responsibility for your own progression.

✓ It's about managing your time in the workplace to achieve your goals.

✓ It's about knowing when to move on and not being afraid to demand something better.

What's it not about?

✖ It's not about accepting your lot and suffering in silence.

✖ It's not about being at the beck and call of everyone else to the detriment of your own progression and sense of achievement.

✖ It's not about moaning constantly or bitching to colleagues until no one wants to work with you.

✖ It's not about bullying subordinates or fawning to superiors to get ahead.

✖ It's not about feeling undervalued but putting up with it, especially when the guy who started after you has just been promoted.

you come up with ways around a problem, you'll earn respect. The alternative is to attempt to do what they've asked and fail — and a domme refuses to court failure.

If you are the boss, make sure that you're there for your staff. But remember, as a manager, your staff are not your friends. It may sound harsh but it's true. No matter how well you get on with them, you need to maintain enough distance that you could sack them without a qualm if they mess up. That doesn't mean that you can't be supportive, friendly, or join in with office socials. Just keep confessions about how cute you think the man who fixes the photocopier is to yourself (and your friends).

And no matter what level you're at, make a point of giving yourself a personal appraisal every year, to help you maintain your dream. Set yourself goals: it could be enrolling in a course to learn new skills, working part-time, getting home from work every day at 5:00 P.M., or saving up enough money to take a career break. By regularly analyzing your career path, you'll feel the progress you're making and undoubtedly end up achieving your dream.

Don't be afraid to ask for advice from people who have achieved their goals. You spend much of your day at work and the trick is always to work smarter not harder.

Quitting and Moving On

Having your value go unrecognized is usually what prompts people to look for different employment. Just make sure you really do want to leave the job you're in. Resigning from a position that dents your self-worth is an empowering feeling. You're in control of your world again, which is the way all confident women live their lives. But if you haven't got a new job lined up, it's natural to feel nervous. Try to turn your fears into positives; feel excited that your future is in your hands. And what a future you've got!

Dominatips

Keep your domme in the back of your mind at all times and your power will grow. You'll ask your boss for that pay raise. You'll never again put up with men who lack respect for women. And your domme will be there with you through everything. Whips at the ready! Off you go!

Index

aggression, dealing with 50–53
apologizing 62
appraisal, personal 110
archetypes 15
attention stealers 37, 43–46
authority, dealing with 48–50

barrier gestures 21, 22
birth position 59
body image 79
body language 20, 22, 52, 71, 72
boundaries 10, 25–27, 34, 98
    in families 58, 60
    in relationships 75–76

children 60
clearing the decks 98–101
clothes 12, 44, 100–101
clutter, clearing 100–101, 104
communication 21, 74
confidence 10, 12, 20, 71, 87
    see also self-confidence
confidence crushers 37, 46–48
conflicts, dealing with 98, 99
control: of others 35
    of self 18–19
conversation 21, 22
counseling 63

dating 66–69
decisiveness 11
domme: accessing 13, 16
    creating 15
    releasing 9

family 57–60
    conflicts with 99
    saying "no" to 23
flattery, using 49–50
friends: making new 56
    money and 54

moving on from 53–56
    pressure from 34–37
    saying "no" to 23

honesty 10, 68, 77
housework 61, 92–93, 101–104

independence 11
insecurity 81

life management 91
listening 55, 71
lover, choosing a 67

money: friends and 54
    managing 94–97
    in relationships 61–62

negatives, eliminating 28–29
networking 107
"no," saying 23–27

partner see relationships
passivity 17, 36, 38, 41–42, 44, 85, 106
personal space 22
Positive Visualization 70
pressure: from friends 34–37
    in relationships 76, 79

rejection, dealing with 68
relationships 60–62, 66–69
    boundaries in 75–76
    ending 85–86
    money and 61–62
    moving on from 83
    problems 81–84
    respect in 66, 77, 78, 84
    sex and 69–72, 76–80
    talking about 81–82

respect 11
    in relationships 66, 77, 78, 84
    at work 106, 108
role models 15
role-play 12–13, 14
routines, assessing 18–19

saying "no" 23–27
seduction 71–72, 74–75
self-actualization 29
self-analysis 28–29
self-belief 16–17
self-confidence 19–22
    see also confidence
self-control 18–19
self-doubt 19, 62, 63
self-esteem 20, 22, 29–30
sex 69–72, 76–80
    safe 77–78
sex drive 70
sexuality, using 61, 71–72
siblings 59
social life 36
STDs (sexually transmitted diseases) 78

temper, keeping 52
time alone 29–31
time-management 43, 54, 90–93, 99
    at work 93, 108
time thieves 37, 38–43
time wasting 43, 99

work: dream job 105–106
    as boss 110
    as employee 106–110
    goals 110
    quitting 111
    saying "no" at 26
    time-management at 93
    work/life balance 90